Substance Use Disorder:

Understanding Its Struggle, Reversing the cycle and Breaking Free

By

Dr.Gerard E. Johnson

Copyright© by Dr.Gerard E. Johnson 2022.All rights reserved.

Before this document is duplicated or reproduced in any manner, the publisher's consent must be gained. Therefore, the contents within can neither be stored electronically, transferred, nor kept in a database. Neither in Part nor full can the document be copied, scanned, faxed, or retained without approval from the publisher or creator.

Table of Contents

INTRODUCTION

The use, misuse, and dependency on drugs and alcohol constitute a global epidemic.Not only are we losing our children to this illness, but also our siblings, parents, friends, and neighbors.Overdose fatalities and the number of productive lives lost to addiction are both on the rise.Addiction includes gradually losing control over usage.At this point, terrible things will probably start to occur.Over time, the brain is altered by these substances having an impact on its structure and function of.Because of this, medical professionals view drug use disorder as a brain illness.Making the decision that you've had enough or can't do this on your own is essential for a successful detox from drug abuse.Using drugs or alcohol can affect your sense of judgment and make it more complicated for you to think clearly.This book provides the necessary informations and coping mechanisms needed to deal with the use of alcohol and drugs by enlightening and reinforcing your drive to do so successfully.

CHAPTER 1
EXPLAINED: SUBSTANCE USE DISORDER

When a person becomes dependent or relies heavily on a substance, be it alcohol or drugs in this context to function in everyday life, they tend to abuse these substances because they cannot control their urges and typically use the substance more often over time.It is a neurological disorder that impairs a person's capacity to regulate the use of either prescribed or illicit drugs.Alcohol, marijuana, nicotine e.t.c all directly stimulate the brain's reward system initiating pleasurable sensations. People may have acute cravings for the drug due to its intense activation in the brain.Making these persons liable to skip out on routine tasks.If you are hooked, you could use the substance even when it is harmful.The young adult population is more susceptible to this problem. First-time experiences are frequently motivated by:

- To feel high" or "intoxicated
- To relax, forget about issues, or experience numbness.
- To perform or think better.

- Experimentation, curiosity, and peer pressure
- injury treatment.

Addiction is another name for substance use disorder.

People are also vulnerable to drug addiction when exposed to or obtain medications from a friend or relative who was solely prescribed the medication, especially with opioids.Each substance possess diverse levels of addiction perils and speed of addiction development.Opioid medicines for example, have an increased risk and results in substance abuse more quickly than other drugs.

Commonly abused substances include:

- Alcohol
- pharmacological therapy for anxiety and sedation
- Caffeine
- Cannabis (including marijuana and synthetic cannabinoids)
- Inhalants that cause hallucinations, such as LSD, phencyclidine, and psilocybin
- Opioids (including fentanyl, morphine, and oxycodone)

- Stimulants (including amphetamines and cocaine)
- Tobacco

Substance Use Disorder Spectrum
1.Intoxication

The term "intoxication" describes a substance's immediate and transient effects. A person's mental capacity, judgment, and mood may all be affected by alcohol.A person may experience exhilaration, an increased sense of happiness (or euphoria) or they may feel calmer, more relaxed, and sleepier than usual, depending on the substance.

2. Tolerance

This happens when a person's body or brain no longer reacts to prescribed medications or recreational substances as it used to.When someone takes a particular substance for a long time, they frequently develop tolerance to it.The drug dosage is no longer effective as it now activates fewer receptors or enzymes in the body and brain.

This implies that individuals must take more of the drug to get the same results they got at first.Higher dosages raise the danger of overdose as your body develops tolerance.

3.Withdrawal

When a person stops using or reduces the consumption of a substance like alcohol ,prescription or recreational medication, they often suffer withdrawal, which is a mix of physical and mental consequences.Depending on the drug and dose used, different adverse consequences are created.Some substances' withdrawal symptoms (such as those from alcohol or barbiturates) can be severe or fatal and may include;

Changes in appetite, mood, chills or shivering, congestion, depression, fatigue, muscle discomfort, nausea, Sleeping problems and vomiting.In some instances, more severe symptoms, delirium, seizures, and hallucinations may also happen.

Disorders induced by substance use

Disorders brought on by substances are diseases or symptoms that develop as a direct physiological result of intoxication or withdrawal.

1. **Anxiety disorders brought on by substance use**: include symptoms of panic, anxiety, irritability, and sleeplessness.
2. **Addiction-related bipolar disorder**:When drugs are not utilized, the manic highs and dismal lows still exist.
3. **Psychosis brought on by substance misuse** is characterized by auditory, visual, or other hallucinations and delusions that would not typically exist without the presence of the substance in question.
4. **Obsessive-compulsive disorder brought on by drug use:** People who use substances feel forced to carry out pointless behaviors or acts to calm their anxiety, such as locking doors many times before leaving the house or washing their hands twice before leaving the bathroom.

5. **Sexual dysfunction brought on by drug addiction** refers to problems with arousal, desire, orgasm, or pain that are far worse than the usual libido-damaging consequences of substance abuse.
6. **A drug-induced sleep disorder** is characterized by sleep disruptions, such as hypersomnia or insomnia, which don't often happen when a substance isn't being taken.
7. **Substance-induced neuro-cognitive disorders:** Substance misuse results in poor cognitive function, including aphasia, memory loss, and speech problems.

Assessment of substance use disorder

Possible Signs or behaviors to exhibited for drug addiction to be diagnosed

- Wanting to quit using the substance persistently and attempt to limit or regulate substance usage continually

- continuing to use the substance while being aware that it probably caused or makes mental health problem worse
- showing signs of withdrawal while not utilizing the chemical
- attempting to get the material, use it, or recuperate from using it for a prolonged period
- developing a tolerance to the point that more of the drug is required to have an impact
- an intense desire to utilize the drug
- using despite being unable to complete obligations relating to the job, education, or your home
- using the substance although it creates or exacerbates interpersonal issues
- Continue using the drug even in potentially hazardous conditions, such as when driving under the influence of alcohol or a toxic narcotic.
- spending money on the medication despite not being able to afford it
- stealing or engaging in other actions you wouldn't ordinarily undertake to obtain the substance

Possible signs that your child or another member of your household is taking drugs include:

Issues in job or school: frequent absences from school or work, a sudden loss of interest in work or school activities or reduced grades or performance at work/School

Physical ailments: Lack of drive and enthusiasm, weight increase or loss or red eyes

unkempt appearance: Lack of concern for appearances, grooming or attire

Behavior modifications: Exaggerated attempts to keep family members out of his or her room, secrecy around where one travels with pals, or abrupt changes in behavior and interactions with loved ones

Money problems: Unexpected demands for money without a good cause, the finding of lost or stolen money, or the disappearance of goods from your house that may be used to fund drug use, are all warning flags.

Risk Factors of Substance use

The abuse of drugs and addiction to them may harm anybody, in the world.

Irrespective of their gender, race, or ethnicity.But several factors makes it more likely for someone to be diagnosed with a drug use disorder.Genetics is a significant factor in addiction, as they are with many other diseases.The following are additional risk factors for developing drug abuse problems:

- sexual, mental, or physical abuse
- exposure to trauma
- Access to drugs from family members or classmates who use or abuse substances
- illnesses of the mind, such as sadness, anxiety, and personality disorders

CHAPTER 2
THE BRAIN SCIENCE OF ADDICTION

Drug addiction and the neurology of reward.

The human brain is programmed to reward us whenever we perform pleasurable activities.This incites the release of the neurotransmitter **DOPAMINE**.Addiction is more than just a poor habit; it's a brain alteration that interferes with common sense and willpower.Drug or alcohol addicts will put their addiction before their career, family, or even their fundamental survival instincts. The "reward" circuit, whose primary centers of activity are in the ancient brain region known as the limbic system, is the route at the core of all addictions.This route is also present in "addictions" that do not involve drugs, such as obsessive and harmful behaviors related to eating, exercising, gambling, or having sex.

Neurotransmitters are substances that allow signals to go from one neuron to another through the spaces (synapses) that separate them.The primary neurotransmitter in the brain reward system is dopamine.Electric commands are sent out from cell bodies in the ventral tegmentum.They leap down the cells' cable-like axons to their terminals in the nucleus accumbens, where dopamine is ejected into the synapses.

When dopamine is discharged into synapses, it doesn't stay there for long before being sucked back up by the presynaptic neuron's transporter. Addictive medicines alter how dopamine is usually handled, extending its stay in synapses and the pleasant sensations it causes.Some drugs push the presynaptic cell to release more dopamine than usual.Others work by inhibiting the transporter's ability to reabsorb dopamine; some may even combine these two methods.Cocaine, for instance, can attach to the transporter and prevent dopamine reuptake due to its ability to mimic dopamine so effectively.Amphetamines also alter the transporter's typical action, inhibiting reuptake but simultaneously employing it to push more dopamine from the presynaptic cell into the synapses.

This not only boosts our mood but also motivates us to carry on with our actions.Our brains will also learn to repeat this activity as a result.

Although not everyone who uses drugs becomes hooked in this way.If you are already at risk, here is where the addiction cycle might start.

Cravings are another effect of addiction.These desires can be distressing, persistent, and disruptive. Additionally, going through a drug withdrawal is a physically terrible experience.When the drug is not taken, people experience mental or bodily suffering. Since substance usage is the only thing that alleviates the unpleasant withdrawal symptoms, users are often driven to use substances to escape this pain.Once hooked, a person's primary needs are to satisfy cravings and prevent withdrawal.These individuals use drugs to feel normal, not good. Patients with drug use disorders exhibit alterations in brain regions essential for judgment, decision-making, learning and memory as well as behavior control.These modifications affect how the brain functions and explains why addictive behaviors are obsessive and harmful.

Addiction Cycle

You can avoid going too far down the path to full-blown addiction by being aware of how your brain and body change as you progress through the many phases of addiction.

In this instance, addiction develops in phases and, like other chronic disorders, frequently spirals into a cycle of addiction.Addicts and their families will find it helpful to comprehend the steps of addiction rehabilitation.Every level explains how to identify the issue, accept it, prepare for addiction therapy and deal with alcohol and drug usage following treatment.

Stage 1: Initial Use

Calming down, relieving tension or assistance in managing mental or physical discomfort. Regardless of the initial motivation for using drugs or drinking alcohol, most people never set out to develop an addiction.Unfortunately, for some people, using drugs once or occasionally can lead to a downward cycle of usage and reliance that they are powerless to stop.This applies to using alcohol and drugs recreationally as well.

People may use prescribed painkillers but then switch to illegal narcotics when they can no longer acquire their regular meds.No matter how the first usage occurs, it is the first step toward addiction.

Stage 2: Common or Social Use

The person has moved past their first use of drugs or alcohol at this point in their addiction.They now consistently utilize them, making it a habit.But not sufficient to qualify as a drug use disorder. Although some people may be able to take drugs regularly without forming a dependence, the risk of substance misuse significantly increases during this period.It is crucial to watch out for changes in mood and behavior, changes in priorities or early physical signs of addiction during this stage.

Stage 3: Dangerous Use/Abuse

In stages 1 and 2, positive reinforcement can make someone advance to stage 3.In this stage, the drug user starts to prioritize drug usage above other aspects of their lives and either loses awareness or becomes unconcerned with the effects of their actions.

Their interpersonal connection deteriorates, they encounter difficulties at work, face legal issues and may take part in risky activities that endanger both theirs and others' safety.The drug is now the body's reward, and as a result, the body will start to want it, leading to more intense usage and subsequent recurrent use.In stage 4, addiction and complete reliance are readily enabled by the physical requirement for the substance and the psychological need.

Stage 4: Drug addiction and chemical dependencies

The body or brain eventually depends on the drug to operate correctly.At this time, drinking or taking drugs is no longer a choice; one must do so to avoid experiencing withdrawal symptoms.At this stage of addiction, mental health frequently deteriorates as alcohol or drug dependency harms the general quality of life.When drugs and alcohol are used often, the brain's function begins to alter.The brain will eventually quit producing the neurotransmitters required to control emotions and other body processes waiting on the drug to control these actions.

As a person uses a substance repeatedly, their body will build tolerance to it and needing higher doses more frequently to provide the same results.

Stage 5: Addiction and Substance Use Disorders (SUDs)

Full-blown addiction is the last stage.When a person no longer questions their increasing substance use and is at ease with the danger, risk, and obstacles they have added to their lives.Most of the person's thoughts will be on when and how they may get high once more.They could forgo eating, sleeping and practice poor hygiene.Their personal and professional lives will suffer.

In Spite of all this, no matter how long a person has struggled with drug addiction, support is always accessible.

CHAPTER 3
TYPES OF SUBSTANCE USE DISORDERS

1.Alcohol Use Disorder

This is a chronic, recurrent brain illness also called severe AUD.It is defined by compulsive alcohol use, a lack of control over alcohol use and emotional feeling when not drinking.

Effects and Health Consequences

1. injuries caused by falls, drownings, car accidents and burns.
2. Violence, such as homicide, suicide, sexual assault, violence against intimate partners
3. risky sexual practices, like having sex without protection or with several partners. These activities can result in unwanted pregnancy or sexually transmitted infections, including HIV.
4. Miscarriage, stillbirth and fetal alcohol spectrum disorders (FASDs) among pregnant women.
5. Digestion issues, liver illness, high blood pressure, heart disease, and stroke.
6. Breast, mouth, throat, esophagus, larynx liver, colon, and rectum cancer are all examples of this.
7. Mental health challenge
8. Social issues, such as those involving the family, the workplace, and unemployment.

2. Opioid Use Disorder

Opioid is a category of drugs that includes heroin, which is prohibited, as well as **fentanyl, oxycodone, hydrocodone, codeine, morphine** and other prescription painkillers.These medications interact with opioid receptors on nerve cells in the body and the brain and share similar chemical properties.

The natural ingredient **Morphine** is extracted from the opium poppy plant's seed pod and is used to make heroin.Also, a solid synthetic opioid analgesic with 50–100 times the potency of morphine is **Fentanyl.**

This illicitly produced fentanyl that is responsible for the sharp increase in overdoses is sometimes swapped for or combined with heroin, as well as in fake prescription drugs that look like other, less deadly opioids.

How it works

Opioid painkillers are safe when used as directed by a doctor for a brief time.They are liable to be misused as they elicit euphoria.When misused, they can be snorted, injected, taken in more significant doses than recommended or used without a doctor's prescription.In most situations where opioids are taken as directed by a doctor, dependency, addiction, overdose and even death are likely to occur.Since heroin is frequently more readily available and less expensive on the black market, some users have converted from prescription opiates to heroin.Overdose risk is increased due to heroin's fluctuating purity and other substances added in (like fentanyl) on the black market.

Effects and Health Consequences

Opioid receptor proteins, which are present on nerve cells in the brain, spinal cord, gastrointestinal tract, and other organs of the body, are attached to and activated by opioids.

The transmission of pain signals is inhibited when these medicines bind to their receptors especially when provided in methods that aren't intended or at larger doses than recommended; in addition to these side effects, opioids can cause disorientation, nausea, constipation, and respiratory depression.These medications risk addiction since they also affect reward-related brain areas.

1. Repeated opioid use alters how the brain works, causing hormonal imbalances and long-lasting alterations in brain circuits that are difficult to undo.Heroin use is connected to white matter degeneration in the brain, which may have an impact on one's capacity for making decisions, controlling behavior, and responding to stressful situations.
2. Heroin also quickly causes physical dependence and tolerance.

3. When a drug user develops physical dependence, the body becomes used to its presence and experiences withdrawal symptoms when use is abruptly decreased. Within a few hours of the final dose, withdrawal symptoms might manifest.

4. The symptoms of "cold turkey" include restlessness, muscle and bone aches, sleeplessness, diarrhea, vomiting, and goosebumps.

3. Nicotine Use Disorder

The leaves of tobacco plants harvested for use in tobacco products are dried and fermented.Nicotine is an addictive component of tobacco, which is why so many tobacco users have trouble quitting. Tobacco products also include additional compounds that may increase their propensity for addiction.

What do they do?

It can be readily delivered into the body through cigarettes and more recently, via e-cigarettes or "vapes" where nicotine quickly reaches its peak blood levels and enters the brain.

When tobacco is not breathed, it can be absorbed through the mucosal membranes, as in cigars, pipes and smokeless tobacco devices, reaching peak levels more gradually.

Effects and Health Consequences

1. Nicotine activates the adrenal glands, which causes epinephrine to be released (adrenaline). The body is stimulated by this adrenaline surge, causing a spike in heart rate, blood pressure, and respiration.

2. Acute myeloid leukemia, bladder, kidney, mouth, throat, larynx, esophagus, stomach, pancreas, cervix, and kidney malignancies are all linked to smoking.Smokers generally experience twice as many cancer deaths as non-smokers.
3. Smoking during pregnancy increases the risk of miscarriage, stillbirth, early birth, and low birth weight babies.
4. Young people are more susceptible to nicotine,making it easier to acquire hence the tobacco use problem.

Cannabis Use Disorder

The dried leaves of the cannabis plant, that contains the psychoactive substance delta-9-tetrahydrocannabinol (THC) and other related chemicals, are referred to as marijuana.

Effects and Health Consequences

1. When marijuana is smoked, THC enters the circulation swiftly from the lungs and travels to the brain and other organs.THC is absorbed by the body more gradually when the plant is chewed.This affects brain receptors that typically respond to naturally occurring THC which are essential for proper brain growth and function. The "high" that marijuana induces as well as other effects like hallucinations, delusions, psychosis, altered senses, difficulty with attention and problem-solving, impaired memory, and elevated heart rate are all caused by marijuana's over-activation of parts of the brain that contain the highest number of these receptors.

2. Like smoking tobacco, using marijuana can lead to respiratory issues such as frequent coughing up phlegm and an increased risk of lung infections.

3. The consumption of marijuana during pregnancy is associated with lower birth

weight and a higher risk of cognitive and behavioral issues in the fetus.

4. Some marijuana long-term usage has been associated with mental diseases, including worsening symptoms in those with schizophrenia and bipolar disorder and higher rates of depression and social anxiety disorder.

4. STIMULANTS USE DISORDER

Cocaine and methamphetamine are examples of stimulants, as are certain prescription drugs like Ritalin, Adderall, Modafinil and others.Cocaine is a substance that is extracted from the coca plant in South America.It frequently appears as a fine, white, crystalline powder when sold as a street drug.Crack is cocaine that has been transformed into rock crystals.Heat and smoke are applied to the crystals. Methamphetamine often comes in the shape of a tablet or a white, bitter-tasting powder that readily dissolves in water.Another type of stimulant known as "crystal methamphetamine" appears as sparkling, bluish-white pebbles or glass pieces.It is sometimes called crystal, meth, chalk, or ice.

What do they do?

Before now, stimulants were used to treat conditions such as obesity, neurological diseases, asthma and other respiratory issues.However, the medicinal usage of stimulants decreased when it became clear that they can be abused and addictive.Only a small number of medical disorders, including ADHD, narcolepsy and occasionally depression in patients who have not responded to conventional therapies, are now treated with stimulants.

Cocaine and methamphetamine occur in many forms and can be smoked, snorted, eaten, or injected.The method of administration affects the drug's duration and potency.

The speed with which some techniques (including smoking and injection) enter the circulation increases the drug's potential for addiction, the risk of overdose and other adverse health effects.

Effects and Health Consequences

1. Stimulants work therapeutically by slowly and steadily increasing dopamine in the same manner that dopamine is created in the brain naturally.

2. Prescription stimulants can stimulate brain dopamine more significantly and faster when taken in amounts and other than those recommended (similar to illegal stimulants like methamphetamine), resulting in pleasure and raising the risk of addiction.Increased energy and talkativeness, as well as a decreased hunger and desire for sleep, are other short-term impacts of stimulant abuse. Large doses can result in unpredictable and occasionally aggressive behavior.

3. Cardiovascular consequences, such as irregular heartbeat and heart attacks; neurological effects, such as headaches, seizures, strokes and coma.

4. And also, gastrointestinal difficulties such as nausea and stomach discomfort are some of the most common medical complications linked to stimulant overdose.

5. Cocaine is harmful and increases the risk of overdose when combined with other substances, such as heroin or alcohol.

5.HALLUCINOGEN USE DISORDER

A wide range of substances known as hallucinogens that distorts perception (consciousness of surroundings, objects, and situations), thoughts and feelings. Hallucinations are sensations, sounds, and sights that appear real but are not.. Some plants and mushrooms (or their extracts) contain hallucinogens and can also be produced in the laboratory.

What do they do?

There are several methods to consume hallucinogens, including smoking, snorting, and absorbing them via the tongue lining.

The effects of hallucinogens can start to take effect in as little as 30 to 90 minutes and linger for 6 to 12 hours.Trips are the usual name for hallucinogen-induced experience.

Effects and Health Consequences

1. Hallucinogens momentarily stifle the spinal cord's and brain's chemical connection.
2. It also interferes with the brain's chemical serotonin, which controls mood, sensory perception, sleep, appetite, body temperature, sexual behavior, and muscle control.
3. The brain neurotransmitter glutamate, which controls pain perception, environmental reactions, emotion, learning, and memory, is interrupted by other hallucinogens.
4. Extreme and irrational distrust of people known as paranoia and separated thought from reality is known as psychosis.
5. Ketamine users may experience memory loss, renal issues, and bladder ulcers. Speech issues, memory loss, weight loss, anxiety, sadness, and suicidal thoughts are a few of these side effects

CHAPTER 4
TEENAGE DRUG ABUSE

Teenagers are more likely to experiment with drugs than adults.This is because their minds are not yet completely matured as they lack the same decision-making capacity unlike adults.This is because, the area of the brain(prefrontal cortex) responsible for reasoning and making decisions is less active throughout this time.So, they are vulnerable to problems of substance abuse. Teenagers are more inclined to attempt drugs throughout adolescence since it is a period where they engage more in risky behaviours.The brain at this phase is built for taking risks.

There are lots of obstacles that will need to be dealt with in the upbringing of teens and also in the teenage hood phase of life.For many teenagers, using and abusing illegal substances is normal.Drug use in adolescence is a risky prospect, even if most teenagers who take drugs do not go on to become drug abusers or addicts in adulthood.

Alcohol, marijuana and inhalants are only a few examples of substances that can be abused to varying degrees and cause harm.Typically, the areas of life where drug use and misuse have the most significant impact are school and family relationships.

What leads young people to take drugs?

Teenage drug and alcohol usage issues are as a result of many different factors.Substance misuse doesn't start as full-blown abuse or addiction; it develops over time.Different routes or pathways might lead to a teen's drug misuse problem.

The following are risk factors of teenage drug abuse:

- Inadequate parental oversight and monitoring
- Parents and children don't engage or communicate enough
- Rules and expectations prohibiting substance use that are unclear and poorly stated
- Family conflicts include parents or family members who take drugs,
- Childhood maltreatment or neglect
- Peer pressure to use drugs, bullying and gang membership
- Disorders like ADHD or depression.

It's not a guarantee that someone will get addicted even if they have one or more risk factors. However, the possibility that substance use will lead to abuse or addiction increases as more risk factors are present.

The following should be implemented to save any child from this menace

- Discuss drugs with your children frequently,
- give them access to positive role models,
- encourage them to get involved in a faith-based organization
- Build a close relationship with your adolescent, and instill in them the idea that drugs are dangerous and that addiction frequently necessitates lifelong care and therapy.

CHAPTER 5
ADDICTION THERAPIES

Can a person with addiction be helped?

Although there is no precise cure for addiction, it is treatable.In other words, when a person stops engaging in their addictive activity for a while, their addiction might go into remission, but it can reappear.Relapse rates for addictive disorders are regrettably reasonably high, making those with a history of addiction particularly susceptible to them. There are techniques for managing moderation depending on the addiction, its intensity, and the history of the person's connection with their addiction.Many people can live fulfilling lives while controlling their addictive behavior. Abstinence-based methods of treatment, in which one can abstain entirely from the addictive activity, are sometimes used and are more commonly acknowledged by the addiction recovery community and addiction professionals.

What are the remedies for drug abuse?

Recognizing that a person's substance use has turned into a problem that is impairing their quality of life is the first step on the road to recovery.

Impairment in crucial areas of function, such as job, education, social interaction and enjoyment may cause this.There are many different treatment options available once someone realizes how detrimental substances are to their lives.

The kind of addictive condition, the duration, intensity of use and the impact of addiction on the person involved are just a few of the variables that affect treatment choices for addiction.A physician will also take care of any health challenge, such as liver illness in an individual with alcohol addiction or lung problems in an individual with smoking addiction.Several treatment alternatives are available and most addicts undergo a mix of this methods.All available therapies for addictive illnesses don't work for everyone.Common interventions include **inpatient and outpatient programs, psychological therapy, self-help groups, and medication.**

Treatment options for drug use disorders range widely.Treatment is beneficial, even for severe cases.One can frequently receive a mix of these treatments:

Detoxification

Usually, detoxification comes first in a therapy plan. Limiting withdrawal symptoms and removing the drug from the body are involved.A person who is dependent on many substances will require medication to ease the symptoms of withdrawal from each.

Depending on the person's needs, therapy may be provided in a group, a family or an individual setting.The initial phase of treatment is often vigorous, with the number of sessions progressively decreasing as symptoms improve.

The various forms of therapy include:

- **Cognitive-behavioral therapy**:Assists individuals in identifying and altering thought patterns that are linked to substance abuse.
- **Multidimensional family therapy** is intended to enhance family functioning in the

presence of a teen or teenager with a drug use disorder.

- **Motivational interviewing** increases a person's willingness to modify their behavior.
- **motivating rewards that promote abstinence via gratification**
- **The goal of addiction counseling is to assist** clients in changing their attitudes and behaviors related to substance use.It also attempts to improve clients' life skills and support other therapies.
- **Therapies with medication assistance:**The use of medication during detox can reduce cravings and ease withdrawal symptoms.

Rehabilitation programs

Programs for substance-related and addictive disorders that are longer-term can be pretty successful and usually have a strong emphasis on maintaining drug-free status as well as resuming function within the social, career, and familial duties.

Residential facilities that are fully licensed are ready to set up a 24-hour care program, give a secure living space, and provide any required medical interventions or help.

Different facilities that offer therapeutic settings includes:

- **Residential short-term treatment** focuses on detoxification and preparing a person for a longer time in a therapeutic community through rigorous counseling.
- **Therapeutic communities:** For six to twelve months, a person receiving long-term therapy for a severe type of addiction would dwell in a home with staff members working there and other people in recovery. The community and staff significantly influence recovery from drug use and modifications in attitudes and behaviors related to drug use.
- **Recovery housing:** This type of housing offers a short-term, supervised stay to assist residents in adjusting to new responsibilities and a life free from ongoing substance use.

- Rehabilitation housing connects a person in the latter phases of recovery with community support services and offers help managing finances and obtaining employment.These could enable the recovered person to connect with others who share their addiction, which frequently increases motivation and lessens feelings of loneliness.Additionally, they may be a good source of information, community and education.

Preventions

Can I stop drug abuse before it starts?

Yes. Education is the first step in preventing drug addiction.Education in families, communities and schools can stop first-time substance abuse.Additional measures to stop drug abuse include:

- Never attempt illicit drugs even once.
- Observe the directions on any prescribed medicine.Never take more than is recommended.For instance, addiction to opioids can begin barely five days after use.

- To lower the chance of medicines being abused by others, quickly dispose of unneeded medications.

Does any circumstance increase the chances of drug use disorder?

Many people struggle with both drug use disorders and mental health issues.Sometimes, mental disease exists before the onset of addiction.In other instances, a mental health condition is brought on by or made worse by the addiction.The likelihood of recovery increases with appropriate treatment for both disorders.

Addiction: Does it have long-term effects?

The architecture and functioning of the brain may alter if you continue to abuse drugs.Substance use disorder affects how you behave, manage stress, learn, make judgments and decisions and store memories.

Can an addiction recur?

A "relapsing sickness" is analogous to substance use disorder.People recovering from this illness have a higher likelihood of resuming drug use.

A relapse might still occur many years after your last drug use. You will require continued care due to the chances of relapsing.Your healthcare professional should discuss your treatment plan and modify where necessary to meet your evolving requirements. Inform your medical professionals if you have a problem with prescription medications, particularly opioids.They can aid you in locating other pain-management choices.

Drug addiction: Is it fatal?

Drug use disorders are tragic.One can likely die from an overdose or from engaging in risky activities while under the influence of drugs if you go untreated.Treatment can aid in addiction recovery and help people avoid negative outcomes.

It's difficult to overcome an addiction.A great level of willpower and self-control will be required to establish and sustain long-term sobriety.On this voyage, nevertheless, you are never alone yourself. You'll develop close bonds with others in recovery who understand what you're going through during therapy.During this challenging time, your loved ones, including your family and friends, have your best interests in mind.The amount of work you put into the process will determine how quickly you recover from an addiction.To better comprehend what comes ahead, learn about the many ways addiction is treated .

Addiction's Negative Connotations And Prejudice

"Stigma" describes unfavorable attitudes, conclusions and stereotypes founded on presumptions about a particular group of individuals.It may result in exclusion and unequal treatment, sometimes called "discrimination." People's perceptions of themselves can also be altered by stigma and prejudice; they could start to believe the unfavorable opinions others have stated about them.Self-esteem, mental health and general wellbeing may all be impacted by this.By doing this, therapeutic hurdles are created and these illnesses worsen.Many individuals consider addiction to be a moral or personal failing.

Therefore, even if they are friends or family members, people with drug use disorders may cause them to experience dread and rage.

Many people find it difficult to identify and assist any person suffering from the illness. Everyone in our society, from medical experts and addiction researchers to members of the general public and those directly impacted by drug and alcohol issues, can help lessen stigma and prejudice towards those with substance use disorders.

The Struggle in Addiction

Addicts may have a hard time recovering from this sickness and most people seeking addiction treatment experience at least one relapse.Before finally succeeding, many addicts must make a lot of efforts at rehabilitation.It's crucial to remember that healing is possible as long as the person persists.Nevertheless, no matter how hard they try, some people will find it difficult to break an addiction.

Others won't be able to complete their recovery for several reasons.To have a chance to recover fully, these people must understand why they are constantly battling their demons.

REASONS SOME FAIL

Despite their willingness to seek treatment and wish to stop using, some addicts experience repeated failure.There are various reasons this occurs;

- **Failing to take action after deciding to seek assistance:**Many addicts will have times when they feel ready to seek treatment, but if they don't act, they may discover that their resolve starts to wane and that they quickly revert to their previous methods of satisfying their addiction.Most people may also go through phases where they believe quitting would be better for them and their families, but there are also times when they simply do not want to live without the pleasure their habit provides.These people are unable to embrace the concept of recovery truly.
- **Many addicts struggle to kick out the habit because they don't seek expert assistance:** Some people will try to become well because they think they can stop independently. However, the pull of addiction is frequently too great and they cannot persevere.

- **Another significant barrier to some addicts conquering their afflictions is fear:**Some People think they lack the strength to handle any withdrawal symptoms they may go through.Many people mistakenly feel that these withdrawal symptoms will be far worse than they are and will be too tough to live with.

- **Whether an addict will be successful in their recovery efforts depends on peer pressure:**Peer pressure can play a role in some people developing an addiction in the first place and it can also play a role in some addicts not completing their recovery.Many addicts are reluctant to cut off their relationships with their addict pals, which may deter them from getting assistance.

- **Addicts who fail often do so because they are unhappy with their development.**Many people have irrational expectations about how their rehabilitation will proceed and believe that their life will improve overnight.

They become angry and may conclude that their life was better while they were using it if this does not occur.

How Can I Support Someone Who Is Addicted?

It is usually advised that a person cannot quit using on their own, so others should encourage them to get assistance for their addiction since addictions are chronic, progressive, and sometimes lethal.An intervention may be required if a person resists treatment or is in denial about their addiction. Although there are other types of interventions, the most popular one involves assembling close friends and family to support the addict in persuading them to seek addiction treatment.Family members may be asked to show their love and concern for the addict during the intervention process.Last but not least, regardless of whether the addicted person gets help or not, loved ones must find their sources of support. Family therapy and mutual aid organizations can offer these types of assistance for family members.

METHODS TO ASSIST A PERSON IN REHABILITATION FROM ADDICTION.

1. Discourage friction and pointless disputes.

Family stress can worsen underlying mental health conditions like depression or anxiety and lead to a drug or alcohol relapse.Contribute to the growth of healthy discourse and open communication to aid in the facilitation of constructive assistance.Stay away from unnecessary or unwelcome subjects of conversation and attempt to spend time together doing something nice and vital.

2. Promote healthy habits: Show your support by leading a healthy lifestyle yourself, whether it be via open communication, good sleep hygiene, exercising, eating a nutritious diet, or refraining from drugs, alcohol, and smoking.This has several advantages outside only helping your loved one, as it will enhance your own mental, bodily, and spiritual health.It can also help you and your loved one in recovery connect and heal.

3. Don't pass judgment: People in drug and alcohol rehabilitation are frequently faced with a lot of guilt and shame in the past and may still be harboring unfavorable thoughts about themselves.

They don't need to be judged to make them feel worse. Accept, love, and value people for who they are rather than passing judgment on them. They have undoubtedly traveled far.

4. Encourage and support them: Express your pride in your loved one's recovery to encourage and support them. Simple words of support and encouragement may make a big difference. Encourage them to participate in counseling, addiction recovery programs, mutual aid organizations, and other recovery-related activities.

5. Develop patience: Recognize that nothing happens overnight.Even if someone is in recovery, they may still participate in harmful habits or make bad choices.Recovery involves much more than avoiding drugs and alcohol; it will take time for you to recover and grow.Relapses and other setbacks do occur, too.If they do, continue to be patient with yourself and your loved one while expressing your love, care, and support.

6. Become knowledgeable about addiction and recovery: Recognize that addiction is neither a moral shortcoming nor a problem of willpower.Addiction is an illness that takes over the brain's reward system, interferes with the area of the brain in charge of control, and creates memories and neural connections with the person's addictive behavior. As a result, even seemingly insignificant events may trigger the person's addictive behavior. Relapse rates are, unfortunately, high.

8. Check in on them and actively listen: It's more crucial than ever to check in on your loved ones to see how they're doing and feeling, especially in the COVID-19 era, when many people feel lonely. Everybody desires and needs to be heard. Whenever a loved one confides in you, ensure you are attentive and interested. To prove you understand them and demonstrate that you are paying attention to them, show care and rephrase what they have said. Despite your disagreement, acknowledge their sentiments.

9. Establish appropriate boundaries. Poor boundaries frequently develop during active addiction and may persist after recovery. Everyone must examine their own enabling, codependency, and other problematic habits. This is in everyone's best interest who is participating.

10. Lower environmental stressors Avoid storing drugs or alcohol at home, and refrain from using

them yourself. If you consume alcohol, be careful not to do so in the presence of a loved one abusing it. If you take prescription drugs, keep them hidden from your recovering loved one and locked away. Avoid putting them in settings where they might relapse, or accompany them to help them stay accountable.

Conclusion

We can start the process of comprehending addiction and how it impacts people once we have a more profound knowledge of the underlying science of addiction. To better assist affected people in receiving therapy, this aids in discovering, developing, and understanding the novel and existing treatment options. Because addiction is a complicated illness, we need to have a solid understanding of what we are up against to assist individuals who are suffering effectively.

www.ingramcontent.com/pod-product-compliance
Lightning Source LLC
Chambersburg PA
CBHW070608160726

48003CB00005B/2160